An Inner
Journey to
Christmas

For
Ellie
Chloe
Lilly
and
Keegan

An Inner Journey to Christmas

AN ADVENT DEVOTIONAL

Anne Kathryn Killinger

with a
Christmas Monologue
by John Killinger

CHALICE
PRESS
ST. LOUIS, MISSOURI

Bible quotations, unless otherwise noted, are from the *New Revised Standard Version Bible,* copyright 1989, Division of Christian Education of the National Council of the Churches of Christ in the United States of America. Used by permission. All rights reserved.

Cover art: iStockphoto, BIGSTOCK
Cover and interior design: Elizabeth Wright

www.ChalicePress.com

10 9 8 7 6 5 4 3 2 1   11   12   13   14   15

Print: 978-08272-16389
EPUB: 978-08272-16396 • EPDF: 978-08272-16402

**Cataloging–in–Publication Data is available from
the Library of Congress**

Printed in the United States of America

Contents

Foreword

What were W. B. Yeats' famous words about how the world "slouches toward Bethlehem to be born" every Christmas?

They have always expressed what I feel about this special time of the year.

For me, it usually begins about the middle of November, as the days grow shorter and the nights grow colder.

After Thanksgiving it hits me with full force: Christmas is coming! The anniversary of Christ's birth is almost here again.

Whatever has happened during the year—vacations, illnesses, setbacks, advances—doesn't really matter now. Everything will be changed by the arrival of Christmas and a fresh remembering of Christ's incarnation.

During the weeks before Christmas, I become very meditative. Life shifts into a slower, more deliberate gear. I feel the pull of the past. No, not the pull, the push, the joy, the motivation. I recollect things that inspire me.

The meditations in this little book are some of the overflow from these recollections. They are what I have felt the need to write down, the way a poet sets down the product of reflections about things, the way a cook shares the food from his or her kitchen. They are very simple, everyday things. Things I naturally think of at Christmas.

I hope you like them. They are my gift to you.

Advent

> And the Word became flesh and lived among us.
> – *John 1:14*

Advent is my favorite time of year, for it sets the whole new church year in motion with a great celebration. Weeks in advance of its arrival, church staffs and volunteers begin planning special programs and events. Flower committees meet to design stunning new decorations. Children come in after school and don their bathrobes and head coverings—and in some cases fake whiskers—to practice the nativity pageant. Crismons and other decorations are lovingly unpacked and checked for any repair work they might require. All the choirs practice their special music. And as recorded music fills the fellowship hall, volunteers gather to make wreaths, swags, and huge red bows for the Hanging of the Greens. An air of excitement reenergizes everybody from the youngest child to the oldest church member!

Advent is also a time of waiting. Children wonder what they will get for Christmas. Adults worry about all the things they have to do before the important day arrives. Ministers and teachers think about how they can make the message of Christ fresh and meaningful after all their previous attempts to do so. The very air seems to be charged with expectation!

Advent is a time of rediscovery—of dusting off old memories, finding old values, recovering friendships, and realizing all over again how important the message of Christmas is in our lives. As we sing the old carols, listen once more to the ancient story of Jesus' birth, and enjoy for another season all the greenery and decorations, we are reminded once again of our deepest humanity and our greatest obligations.

Anne Lamott says in *Traveling Mercies* that it's all about grace, "the force that infuses our lives and keeps letting us off the hook." Grace, she says, is "the help you receive when you have no bright ideas left, when you are empty and desperate and have discovered that your best thinking and most charming charm have failed you."

That's what we all find again at Christmas, that in a world gone awry, where people can't find jobs or pay for their medical care or hold on to the homes they have bought in happier times, there is that ancient grace that is as modern as the morning newspaper and as intimate as the breath in our own lungs. It comes alive again as we gear up for another year of songs and sermons, another season of love and celebration, another time of singing with the angels, "Christ is born!"

Who wouldn't be happy with that?

Prayer: Father in heaven, grant that once more in this Advent season our hearts and lives may be changed by the wonder of Jesus' birth. Amen.

Simplicity

Your decrees are wonderful:
    therefore my soul keeps them.
The unfolding of your words gives light;
    it imparts understanding to the simple.

—*Psalm 119:129–130*

When I was growing up in a small town in Kentucky, my mother and I often went to visit her sister, who lived on the other side of town in the big old house where she and my mother were born. Her name was Virginia, but we called her Jen. Not "Aunt Jen," which somehow would have seemed too formal, but "Jen"—a simple name for a gentle, beautiful maiden lady.

The house was much too big for Jen and, as she was very poor, too expensive to heat. So she kept most of it closed off and lived in only two small rooms. Her bookshelves were lined with worn old volumes handed down from my grandfather, who was an omnivorous reader. An old curio cabinet held interesting bits of china and other treasures that Jen always allowed me to handle, even when I was small.

I loved those visits, especially on winter afternoons when an old coal-oil stove kept the rooms toasty and exuded a friendly aroma. Jen's arms were always stretched wide to offer us warm, generous hugs as we came in from the cold.

December was my favorite time of all.

Jen loved chocolate-covered cherries. Before Christmas she always had a brand new box of them that she would open shortly after our arrival. Carefully lifting out one piece, she would hand it to my mother. Then, repeating this action, she would give me a piece. Finally, she would remove one for herself and close the box. Then she would savor her piece very slowly and deliberately, as if it were a choice morsel from some fabulously expensive chocolate shop.

None of us said anything for a while, as we enjoyed letting the sweet taste linger in our mouths for as long as possible.

Then Jen and Mother would talk, and I would happily explore the books and curios as I listened.

The ritual of the candy was always repeated once or twice during the visit. Each time the silence would descend again, as if we were participating in some exotic sacrament.

As poor as she was, Jen never failed to have a Christmas tree. It was always a small cedar she had cut from somewhere on the property. She would set it by the window and decorate it with bits of cotton, brightly colored ribbon, and silver icicles that danced happily in the air currents.

It was all so simple, and yet so magical.

While I sat quietly on the floor admiring the tree, Jen would read aloud the Christmas story from Luke's gospel. Her voice was sweet and melodic, and I would become so entranced by the story that I actually imagined I was there in the stable with Mary and Joseph and the Baby.

I love the memories of that good, simple time.

Sometimes now my life becomes so filled with stress and busyness that I fail to sense the wonder of simple things the way I did then. I miss that special feeling of wonder, and each year I'm grateful for the coming of Christmas, because it helps me to recapture it again.

Prayer: At this often hectic season of the year, O God, I'm thankful for the memories of simpler times, like the ones when my mother and I visited Jen. They help to redeem my life today, and prepare my heart for Christmas. Amen.

Footprints

> And make straight paths for your feet, so that what is lame may not be put out of joint, but rather be healed.—*Hebrews 12:13*

If my father had lived another three months, he would have been 103 when he died. But he never, in all his many years, learned the art of expressing his feelings. A tall, handsome man, he nevertheless had a gruff disposition that frightened most people. He seldom showed love and gentleness even to those closest to him. He didn't hug or touch his wife or his children.

I don't think I loved him less for this, but I sometimes wished I had a daddy and not merely a father.

I have often wondered, through the years, why he didn't love me. It may have been because I was the seventh child, and a tagalong at that. All my siblings were well on their way to adulthood when I was born. He was probably tired of raising and providing for so many children.

Not long ago, as I was having a cup of tea and feeling reflective, I reconsidered the matter again. Why,

I wondered, was it so difficult for my father to say those three simple little words, "I love you"?

As usual my mind ran aground on the problem. I knew I couldn't solve it. So I sat there in my rocking chair, peacefully finishing my tea. Then I closed my eyes and began to see things in my mind as if I were viewing a TV screen.

I could see the little town where I grew up. It was December, and a heavy snowfall had descended in the night. I was only eight, and my mother worried about how I would get to school, a mile and a half away. We didn't have a car, and even if we had one, the streets were much too slippery for driving.

My father didn't say a word about our dilemma. Mother and I noticed that he didn't leave for work at his usual time. That was odd, because he was obsessed with punctuality and was never late for anything. Finally he said to me, "Let's go." Obviously he planned to see that I got to school.

All bundled up, he and I started up the hill from our house. My little legs soon became buried in the deep snow, and I couldn't move. My father, seeing my difficulty, said, "Walk behind me." He began taking short steps and making large footprints in the snow so I could walk in them.

We went all the way to school that way, which was in the opposite direction from his work.

As I remembered this, sitting there in my rocker, the tears began flowing down my face. I wondered how I could have overlooked this gesture of love and kindness when thinking about my father. He did love me. I just hadn't known how to look for his love.

What does the song say, "Love came down at Christmas"?

Love came down to show us the way, to make the footprints we could follow to eternal life. We mustn't fail to see that.

Prayer: Heavenly Father, please don't let me miss the footprints you have made for me—especially now, at Christmastime. Amen.

Seeing

When the angels had left them and gone into heaven, the shepherds said to one another, "Let us go now to Bethlehem and see this thing that has taken place." —*Luke 2:15*

"How do you see Christ?" was the topic of a sermon I heard several years ago. The preacher was our son. He quoted Wihla Hutson's words in the song "Some Children See Him," which say children the world over see the baby Jesus with a face "like theirs, but bright with heavenly grace."

For me, it was a very thought-provoking sermon. It made me realize there are as many answers to the question "How do you see Christ?" as there are people. Each of us sees Jesus in his or her own unique way.

- The person in pain looks to him as a healer.
- Those with a mind for the future see him as a leader.
- The turbulent personality sees him calming the sea.

- The fun-loving person sees him with a sense of humor.
- The angry relate to his chasing the money-changers from the temple.
- The loving person sees him gathering children into his arms.
- The hungry see him feeding the masses with a few loaves of bread and some small fish.
- The poor see him rebuking the rich for not helping them.

At Christmastime, though, I think we all more or less share a single view of Christ. We don't see him as a monarch or a healer or a feeder. We see him as a baby, as one who has become small enough for us to see and adore him, even though he is the greatest one who ever was or ever will be.

Prayer: Father, however we see Christ now, let us always see his kind and compassionate nature, and let it be reflected in the way we live. Amen.

Trees

"Even now the ax is lying at the root of the trees."
—*Luke 3:9*

At our house, getting a Christmas tree has always been a big production. There are so many things to consider. The height must be exactly right, so that the star on its top barely touches the ceiling. Its branches must be heavy enough to hold the heavier ornaments we have collected from all over the world. It must be exceedingly fresh, for once cut and brought into the house, Christmas trees have been known to reside there long after Christmas has actually come and gone.

Trimming the tree is also highly demanding. The many strings of lights, once untangled, are carefully arranged among the branches. (I don't actually measure the distance from one to another, as my husband claims.) Each of our decorations is lovingly and thoughtfully placed so that the overall effect is aesthetically perfect. We always remember where we acquired them and reflect on the dear friends who gave us some of them across the years. Every year I declare, "This is the most beautiful tree we've ever had!"

One year I had the flu and couldn't attend the numerous activities at our church or any of our friends' dinners and parties. I spent most of the time lying on the den sofa, mesmerized by our tree. It stood tall and dignified, and its glow sent rays of warmth and love throughout the room. The little Christ child lying in his cradle looked up at the wonder of it, and so did the rest of the Holy Family and the animals. Candles burned brightly on the mantel amid branches of holly and pine. A crackling fire on the hearth completed the luxurious sense of welcome and comfort.

Lying there and basking in all this wondrous beauty, I began thinking about the various trees we had had in other years.

I considered the first tree John and I ever had, the year we married. He was still in school. I was working, but we didn't have much money. I think I fussed at him for spending two dollars for a tree, thinking we couldn't afford even that much. We decorated it with popcorn, paper loops, pine cones, and red yarn bows because we couldn't afford any glass ornaments. We had only a couple of cheap strings of lights, the kind that all went out when one did, and they were more often out than not. But I remember thinking it was the most beautiful tree I had ever seen.

We had a tree in Paris when our children were small. In the city, trees proved scarce. We had searched and searched before finding one we liked. It wasn't very tall, but we had a ledge in the living room we could set it on so that it seemed bigger than it was. Again we had few lights and had to resort to homemade ornaments. But miracle of miracles, it too seemed like the most beautiful tree we'd ever had.

Then I smiled at memories of the times in other years when John and our boys had driven out into the country to find cedar trees in some farmer's field. They usually brought back several and put them in different rooms of the house. One year they came home with five tied onto the top of our old station wagon. They also brought back ripped coats and pants from climbing barbed wire fences or getting caught in bramble bushes. Whatever the cost in clothes or effort, it was worth it, because I thought those trees were the most beautiful I'd seen.

As I dreamed about those trees, I began to realize that a Christmas tree is a lot more than glowing lights and glittering tinsel. It dawned on me that it is actually a Tree of Life. Reminding us as it does of the birth of Christ and the life everlasting—that's what the green is about—it is always much more than an ordinary tree. It is an ambassador of love and good will. It sheds its light of hope and joy in every surrounding—even on a woman confined at home with the flu!

> Did Jesus have a Christmas tree?
>   Was it fresh and tall and green?
> Did it stand in the manger by his crib
>   all lovely and serene?
> I hope so, little infant Lord, for you have
>   blessed us all!
> For you have blessed us all![1]

---

[1]From "It Happens Every Christmas," a musical by Anne and John Killinger.

Prayer: In all the Christmas trees I see this year, dear God, help me to see in the loveliness of their branches and decorations the beauty and richness of your kingdom brought home again. Amen.

Candles

It is you who light my lamp;
the LORD, my God, lights up my darkness.
—*Psalm 18:28*

My husband and I live in Virginia, a beautiful state filled with the early history of our nation. It is exceptionally comfortable and inviting during the Christmas season, when many houses have candles burning in the windows just as they did centuries ago. There are few things I enjoy more than driving through the countryside on a December evening and seeing a lone house standing in a valley with candles glowing brightly in all the windows. It is a moving sight.

Several years ago we lived in colonial Williamsburg, where the warmth of the past is still reflected in the natural Christmas decorations of fruit, pine cones, nuts, and greenery. And yes, candles burned each night in every window.

I don't know where or why the custom of burning candles originated. Before the advent of electricity they were probably placed in windows at night to guide family members home when there was no moonlight or there was an unexpected snowstorm. Inns too proved hard to find in those days. Perhaps candles were put in the windows to welcome strangers needing a place to rest.

Wouldn't it have been a joyous sight, back in the eighteenth century, to see candles burning in the windows to guide people to a Christmas party? What fun it must have been to visit friends and family by steady, glowing candlelight!

I wonder if God made Christmas as a candle to light our way to him?

Isaiah said, "The people who walked in darkness have seen a great light" (Isa. 9:2). Matthew, who included that very verse in his gospel, must have believed the light to which Isaiah referred was the birth of Christ. John's gospel records, "The light shines in the darkness" (Jn. 1:5). In another place Jesus refers to himself as "the light of the world" (Jn. 8:12).

Many sermons and poems have been written about Jesus as the light. An unknown author described God's Christmas candle this way: "The light that shines from the humble manger is strong enough to lighten our way to the end of our days."

I find that very comforting, especially as I grow older. Maybe it's why Christmas seems dearer and dearer to me. The world appears to become more and more complicated, and it is harder and harder to find our way. But the blessed light from the manger is still there to guide us, regardless of how dark the world is.

Prayer: Thank you, O God, for the eternal flame of your Son, Jesus. It will always light our way home. Amen.

Gifts

Every generous act of giving, with every perfect gift, is from above. —*James 1:17*

The rush is on! Christmas gift lists grow longer and longer. Or if not longer, at least more difficult. Reporters constantly remind us of how few shopping days remain until Christmas. In a panic we check the gift list again. What does Joe really like? What does Mary need? What can I afford?

Gift giving can become a terrible burden. Somehow it no longer seems enough to give a doll, a tie, a basketball, a bottle of perfume, or a basket of oranges. Each year we try to outgive last year's gifts, and usually end up confused and exhausted.

The first Christmas after my husband and I married we were very poor. How glad I was when I received a small check from my parents. I proudly used it to buy some things for my husband. Nothing special. Only the usual tie, socks, and handkerchiefs, because he really needed them.

Meanwhile he had saved up a little money to buy me a few presents. One was a mop, which I truly needed. Another was a beautiful but inexpensive dresser set—a comb, a brush, and a mirror. The most memorable gift he gave me that Christmas was a booklet of homemade coupons. Being artistic by nature, he had made them with beautiful designs and lettering.

Several coupons were for preparing a meal, washing the dishes, cleaning our apartment, and doing the laundry. Others could be redeemed for a hug or a kiss.

I never used the coupons. That booklet was so special to me that I put it in a scrapbook. I still get it out, more than fifty years later, and smile over those two youngsters who did all they could to give one another a nice Christmas in spite of their lack of means.

Gifts don't have to be gold, frankincense, and myrrh.

The little drummer boy in the legend didn't have anything wrapped in fancy, glittery paper to give the Christ child. The only thing he could give was a tune on his drum. "I'll play my best for him," he said.

The poet Christina Rossetti put it this way:

What can I give him,
Poor as I am?
If I were a shepherd
I would bring a lamb;
If I were a wise man
I would do my part;
But what can I give Him?
I will give him my heart.

Prayer: God, we know, because they are similar to the good and perfect gift you gave us, that the best gifts are always treasures from the heart. Amen.

Improvisation

> Better is a little with the fear of the LORD
> than great treasure and trouble with it.
> —*Proverbs 15:16*

Several years ago my husband and I spent six months in Oxford, England. Our older son, who was in the process of getting a divorce, accompanied us. We arrived in early December, when the temperature was well below normal, the ground was frozen, and the heat in the condo we rented had been shut off for several days. When we entered the place, we felt as if we were stepping into a freezer. Our spirits were crestfallen. At home our minds had been full of fantasies about spending Christmas in England. But stumbling into that cold apartment after an overnight trip from the States made everything seem bleak and cheerless.

The one encouraging thing we encountered before climbing into our beds under stacks of blankets was a note on the kitchen table announcing, "Christmas decorations are in a box under the hall stairs." We all fell asleep thinking about the next day, when we would get out those decorations and turn our new home into a festive wonderland!

That evening, after our naps, we braved the cold and walked several blocks to a Chinese restaurant for dinner. We expected, as we were in the land of Charles Dickens, to find an array of colored lights and greenery along the way. But there were almost none of either. Instead we encountered what is known in England as "frozen fog," a phenomenon that occurs when the temperature gets so low that the moisture in the air congeals on everything—bushes, walls, trees, even the end of one's nose. An hour later, with some hot food inside us, we realized that all three of us were a little less than thrilled with our adventure!

The next morning when we rose and looked outside, we found that we were living in a silvery world. The frozen fog had covered everything—grass, bushes, trees, rooftops, cars, roadways, and sidewalks. In the garden behind our condo each rosebush was an artistic sculpture in silver. We gasped at the sheer beauty of it all.

Our first order of business, once we had had some toast and coffee, was to explore the closet for all those decorations. Alas, the box under the stairs proved to be a shoebox with some little ornaments in it, plus a cardboard tube about twenty inches long that, according to a note on its side, contained our tree. The tree was collapsible, sort of like an umbrella, and fitted into that small tube less than two inches in diameter. We felt crestfallen. But we decided to make the best of it. After all, this was only one Christmas of many. Next year we'd be back home, enjoying our usual tree that brushed the ceiling and all the lights and baubles that were a part of our annual Christmas decorations.

Bundling up with scarves over our faces to ward off the cold, we trudged down into the center of town for supplies. We hadn't gone far before we noticed what a crystal wonderland we were in. Door knockers along the way, many with faces like the one on Ebenezer Scrooge's house in *A Christmas Carol*, sported silvery beards. Holly trees were tinged with sparkling diamonds of frost. Rooftops shone brilliantly, like mirrors, in the sunlight. Everywhere, nature was decorated in magical, breathtaking designs.

In the town center, we discovered a wealth of little shops and boutiques where we bought food, simple gifts, and a few decorations. I was delighted with a British Christmas cake from Marks and Spencer's covered with marzipan icing, for I have always loved marzipan. Trekking homeward with our meager purchases, we decided it was going to be one of our best Christmases ever in spite of the sparseness of everything.

Nightfall comes early—about four o'clock—in wintry Britain. So it was almost dark when we put up our scrawny little artificial tree and hung a single string of lights on it. I made some simple little decorations— circles and stars and tiny packages—out of foil paper, and we hung these on the tree as well. A large poinsettia now adorned the sideboard in the living room, and our small personal gifts were wrapped and scattered around it. The place didn't look like home, but somehow, after our initial disappointment, it all seemed warm and inviting, and we were happy in our new surroundings.

Over the next few days we were reminded that English people fill the streets and bustle about just the way we do at Christmastime back home. We noticed that they also took time to chat with others in the stores and often paused in late morning or afternoon to have a cup of tea and a slice of fruitcake with friends. They attended musical programs in their churches or in one of the colleges of the university. They bantered with the butcher while choosing a cut of meat or with the florist when selecting a bouquet of flowers. Their shopping baskets were frequently crammed with fruit, candies, pies and cakes, and fancy Christmas "crackers" that pop open, with a little gift inside when they're pulled apart.

Looking back on that Christmas now, I realize how rich it was with our skinny little tree from a tube, our single strand of lights, our lone poinsettia, and our simple, inexpensive gifts. We don't ever need opulence and noise and grandeur to celebrate the birth of our Lord. A little crèche scene, some frozen fog, and a Charlie Brown Christmas tree are enough when we're contemplating the greatest event in all of human history.

"O come, let us adore him!"

Prayer: Even when things are scarce around us, O Lord, we are richly blessed. Teach our spirits to soar at the least excuse, through Christ our Lord. Amen.

Heart

"Blessed are the pure in heart."—*Matthew 5:8*

I learned that Bible verse when I was a small child, and I have never forgotten it. Even as a girl I thought it meant that a person should live a good, clean life with a focus on pleasing God.

I was fortunate to have a role model, an aunt who lived with us from time to time. She had the purest heart of anyone I ever knew.

Auntie was badly crippled with arthritis, so that from midlife on she was unable to work or hold a job. At times her pain was almost unbearable. From the time I knew her she could barely walk. Eventually she had to remain in bed and take all her meals there. That single room in my parents' home became her entire world. She rarely left it except to go to the bathroom adjacent to it. Yet her room was never a vale of tears, complaints, or withdrawal. Instead it was a place of perpetual sunshine, joy, and generosity.

Auntie relished visits from friends and other family members. They came to her room to minister to her, but always left with a feeling that they had been ministered to. Although she had only a minuscule amount of money, she continually gave something to her visitors, especially if they were young like myself—fifty cents here and a dollar there, always, at her instructions, to buy ice cream or candy or some other kind of treat. Any gifts people brought her were quickly recycled and given to other recipients. She almost always sent her friends away with a flower, a card, or a little bottle of perfume.

Auntie especially loved Christmas. Sometimes I heard her humming carols in her room as she worked to fashion some little present she was planning to give. She enjoyed receiving Christmas cards and then was always eager to share them and their messages with anyone who came into her room to visit.

Auntie crocheted like a professional. Her gnarled hands were always busy, working at some intricate pattern. I never knew her to skip a stitch. Her pain meant that it took her longer to complete a project, but as soon as she finished one, she gave it to her next visitor with a little homemade card attached to it. I think one reason she loved Christmas so much was that it was a special time of giving, and she found a lot of happiness in sending her visitors off with a handmade doily or a pot holder or something else she had crafted for the occasion.

She was a voracious reader and loved to discuss the influence poets and classical authors had had on society. She loved to read her Bible and often imparted some special verse to someone who came to see her after she had read and memorized it. People frequently sat and complained to her about the state of the world, but she always responded with some comment like, "With all the things that are broken and don't work in our lives, it's still a beautiful world!"

I consider it my good fortune that I still have one of the tablecloths my aunt crocheted. It is in an amazingly intricate pattern and done in the most delicate stitching I have ever seen. I know she spent months and months working on it. Today, long after her death, I still admire her handiwork and thank God that there was a person with such a pure and loving soul in my life.

I doubt if Auntie ever knew the extent of her influence on the people around her. She probably thought of herself as a poor invalid, shut up in a very circumscribed world with little opportunity to affect things one way or another. I know she left an indelible impression on everybody who knew her, the way she did on me. I don't think it ever occurred to her to keep anything for herself. She always wanted to give something to others.

But there was one wish I did sometimes hear her express for herself. "When I get to heaven," she would say, "I want a pair of red shoes, and I want to run and leap all over heaven like a young doe!"

Now, at Christmas, I think of Auntie and hope she got her wish. I can imagine her dancing with the angels, especially at this time of the year. I expect she is still busy making little gifts for those around her. She wouldn't be Auntie if she didn't.

Prayer: Dear God, I hope my Auntie has a pair of red shoes for dancing, If she doesn't, I hope you'll let her have them for Christmas this year. Amen.

Music

Sing praises to the LORD. —*Psalms 30:4*

Neurologists are studying the effect of music on our brains. Among other things, they have already determined that certain kinds of music, regardless of their origins, produce similar results in people's brains wherever they are heard around the globe. For example, a sad song intoned by the Maori tribe in New Zealand will make people feel equally sad in London or New York. And a lively ditty from Ireland invariably evokes a happy, upbeat response from folks in Africa or South America or anywhere else in the world.

Perhaps this is why familiar Christmas carols have such a universal effect on people. Songs about the birth of Christ and the holidays in general always bring joy and hope and encouragement wherever they are sung or played.

Very dear friends of ours were recently afflicted by cancer. The wife had breast cancer and was scheduled for surgery. Shortly before she went in for her surgery, the husband's doctor told him that he had prostate cancer. Suddenly these vital people who had always lived life to the fullest found daily existence a struggle. They needed to set many things in order while they still had time. They had to visit with their children and tell them the disheartening news. They had to put their jobs on hold. Life itself seemed abnormally heavy and difficult to bear.

Both had their surgeries and began the process of recuperation. It was a hard, slow process, and they never seemed to have enough energy to cope with the day's problems.

But then one day, the husband e-mailed us, a funny thing happened. His wife put a Christmas CD on the stereo, and old familiar carols were filling the house—in June!

Suddenly they both began to feel better. They had more energy. Their sense of hope and joy returned. They felt like getting out of the house and going to the store. They wanted to have a party and gather friends around them.

I think I understand. The carols spoke an old, familiar message to their brains. They brought back memories of good and happy times. They reminded them of the birth of Christ, and what his birth means to our lives now, even in the worst of times. They made them feel secure again in their faith, and that made them want to be with their friends and celebrate being alive. The carols had put them in touch again with the spirit of Christmas that knows no single time of the year.

I can't help wondering if people in other parts of the world haven't had similar experiences—if a woman afflicted by cancer in Rio de Janeiro or a man dying of old age in Beijing or a child suffering with swine flu in Mexico heard Christmas carols in the summer and began to feel better, remembering the birth of Jesus and the song of the angels.

I wouldn't be at all surprised.

Prayer: Just thinking about Christmas carols makes my heart beat faster, O Lord. Help me make a joyful noise this Christmas, and all year long as well. Amen.

Ornaments

A word fitly spoken
  is like apples of gold in a setting of silver.
Like a gold ring or an ornament of gold
  is a wise rebuke to a listening ear.
  —*Proverbs 25:11–12*

Over the years, my husband and I have acquired a great number of beautiful Christmas ornaments— so many that my husband teases me, saying I don't really need a tree at all, only a cone of chicken wire for displaying all the decorations. We have glass ones, ceramic ones, plastic ones, metal ones, straw ones, yarn ones, and probably some others I'm not remembering at the moment. Oh yes, there's even one made of hardened dough!

But in spite of this embarrassment of riches, one special decoration always holds a place of distinction for me. It is an ornament we bought shortly after our marriage and have cared for with loving tenderness through the years. It is a glass ball slightly less than two inches in diameter. One half of it is silver colored. The other side is cut away to expose a lovely snow scene—a house nestled in the snow-covered hills, a pine tree, and a beautiful sky behind them. A tiny wreath adorns the door of the house, and candles glitter in the windows. In the very forefront of the cutaway stands a snowman, complete with top hat, broom, and tiny buttons for eyes and nose. It is a magical scene. I can still lose myself in it when I gaze upon its exquisite beauty.

I wonder if God enjoys looking at the world at Christmas the way I enjoy looking at this special ornament. What would God see if he did?

Trees and houses and buildings ablaze with hundreds of tiny lights twinkling like the very stars of heaven?

Fresh, downy snow covering parts of the earth like a plump feather comforter?

A jolly old snowman made by the hands of children whose hearts are filled with the merriment of the season?

Houses where families and friends have gathered to share a meal and give thanks for the coming of Christ?

God must love the world he sees. His only Son was born in Bethlehem to give his life for this marvelous earth and to bring us love, joy, peace and comfort. Wow! That's what it's all about, isn't it?

I love our old ornament, because it is my way of saying, every time I hang it on the tree, "Thank you, God, for the birth of your Son!"

Prayer: Help me to love the whole world, dear Father, the way you love it, and to care about everyone in it with even a small portion of your infinite heavenly compassion. Amen.

Shadows

These are only a shadow of what is to come.
—*Colossians 2:17*

I enjoy all our Christmas cards because they bring love and greetings from dear friends and family, but over the months I soon forget precisely what they looked like. Not so with one card we received last year. It featured a painting of the manger scene similar to that on many cards. Over the scene fell a huge shadow shaped like a cross. The scene made me pause and think. It was as if it said, "All this stuff about the baby's birth is very lovely and romantic, but don't forget that his life is going to lead eventually to betrayal and death on the cross."

When Herod sent out his soldiers to find the Christ child and kill him, God warned Mary and Joseph to take their baby and flee to Egypt. Surely Mary understood that there was something very special about her son, that his coming could produce such fear and anxiety in a monarch. I wonder if she had a motherly premonition that something awful would befall her child. How could she not know? She was visited by an angel even before her child was born. Strangers from the fields and from foreign countries came to pay homage to the baby shortly after he was born. She surely knew that something in his life would eventually take him away from her, that a deep shadow lay over his existence from the moment he was given to her.

Were these among the things Mary is said to have pondered? Did she puzzle over them, wondering how to make sense of what she had heard and seen? Did she worry about the shadow over her son's life, and consider what she might do to help him? Would she later ask herself if she could have done anything to prevent what happened to him? Would she ask if she had been too passive?

I think about this because I could ask the same questions of myself. Something happened in our family that I didn't see coming. I was too busy enjoying the closeness we shared with our children even to think about a shadow that I now realize hovered menacingly over us.

One September day a few years ago our second son told us he had decided that he didn't want to be a part of our family anymore. He had married a very wealthy woman who required all of his love and attention. He was saying good-bye to us to protect his relationship to her. It was heart-wrenching to my husband and me, especially as it meant we could never see our four beautiful grandchildren. The shadow had fallen across our lives.

This experience forces me back to the gospels to look at those moments when Mary felt shut out of Jesus' life. One occasion in particular grasps my attention. Mary came to see Jesus. He was teaching a crowd and healing people inside someone's house. Someone came and told him his mother was there. He said he was busy with his heavenly Father's business and didn't have time to see her. I wonder if she felt crushed when his words were reported to her. Was this part of the shadow to her?

Life isn't all peaches and cream for any of us. Regardless of how charmed we are, moments of sheer agony and despair are bound to come. As the poet said, "Into each life some rain must fall."

Yet somehow that's what the shadow of the cross was about, isn't it? In God's own mysterious way, he sent his only Son to dwell among us and experience the limitations and problems inherent in being human— to dwell under the shadow. And for him the shadow deepened until it became a great cloud of darkness and evil overwhelming him, snuffing out his very life at Calvary.

When it happened, did Mary remember and think about any fears and presentiments she had felt even at the time of his birth? She was a mother, like all mothers, and she knew things—things that no man has probably ever truly known.

Prayer: Thank you, God, for the birth of your Son Jesus, and for his triumph over death and shadows. Help us, in the joy of this Christmas season, to remember the shadows over the lives of people we know and be thoughtful of them. Amen.

Shepherds

"I am the good shepherd. The good shepherd lays down his life for the sheep." —*John 10:11*

Years ago, while my husband and I lived in England, we spent many happy hours exploring the countryside. We bought a book on country walks and loved following the quaint directions it gave for such walks. Sometimes the instructions required us to walk a certain number of paces from a particular rock or tree and to climb a stile over a rock wall, where we would find a path leading toward a distant barn. Occasionally we even had to ford a creek to reach our destination, which was usually an old church or a little pub.

My very favorite time for hiking was during the lambing season. A few times we actually saw little lambs being born. I loved watching the young lambs gamboling over the fields after they discovered how to use their legs. I knew they were dancing to tunes only they could hear.

Soon after birth each lamb was marked somewhere on its back with a spot of dye—red or blue or yellow or green. I was told that the colors made it easier for shepherds to round up their own flocks when they became mixed with others in the unfenced pasturelands.

Maybe those shepherds in the gospel of Luke had been rounding up their sheep the night the angel appeared to them. It must have been a startling experience for them. Yet they eagerly left their flocks to search for the baby who would someday be called the Lamb of God.

They probably had no idea that the special baby they visited that night would himself grow up to become a shepherd, one who would know and call his own sheep by name, and who, if he lost a sheep, would diligently search for it until it was found. One who would carry the little lambs in his arms and who in the end would lay down his very life for his flock.

How wonderful that he who was born as a little lamb would one day become the greatest shepherd of all times!

Prayer: Dear Lord, thank you for the dye spot by which you recognize me. I'm so happy to know I shall always be safe in your fold. Amen.

Humor

Then Abraham fell on his face and laughed.
—*Genesis 17:17*

I cannot begin to count the number of Christmas pageants, musicals, and hangings of the greens I have directed, participated in, or merely attended through the years. Most of them were gems, I'm happy to say. But even the worst of them could still pass muster because they were redeemed by unexpected, and often humorous, developments.

One memory of a Christmas pageant stands out vividly from the rest. It took place in a small church in Nashville. An older friend of ours was playing the role of Joseph, leading a fifteen-year-old Mary down the center aisle, pausing at every third or fourth pew to knock on the end of it. Each time he knocked, he asked the same question: "Do you have a room?" The person sitting closest to the end was supposed to respond, "Sorry, there's no room." Then he and Mary would proceed a little way and repeat the performance.

About halfway to the front of the church, Joseph knocked on a pew and asked, "Do you have a room?" A friend of his who was a bit of a card was occupying the nearest seat. "Yes," he responded in a voice loud enough to be heard several pews away, "I can let you have two nice rooms with a view."

Startled at this response, Joseph replied in a voice loud enough to be heard even further than his friend's, "The hell you can!" Nobody was offended by this spontaneous reply. In fact, so much giggling and laughter erupted that the pageant had to be delayed until our friend and his little Mary could recover their bearings.

I think, too, of a Christmas when I was a teenager. A nice lady named Mrs. Tandy was in charge of our church's decorations committee. She and her companions worked extremely hard to make each year's Christmas decorations more special than the ones the year before. On this particular occasion, they labored to get everything in place for the special cantata performed a week or two before Christmas. Everyone said they outdid themselves. The church was so spectacularly beautiful that those drifting into the sanctuary breathed out audible oohs and ahhs.

A great deal of the decorating had focused on the chancel area. A large wooden frame had been erected in the baptistry behind the choir loft to hold a gajillion poinsettias and pots of evergreens. I remember how grand it looked as our choir approached on the night of our big performance. The very sight of it seemed to elicit more volume and passion from the singers.

The program was going well. Everybody seemed to be singing with extraordinary zest. It was going to be the best cantata any choir had ever presented in our church. Then suddenly, halfway through the program, we heard a horrendous cracking noise behind us, followed by a resounding crash.

The wooden frame had broken under the weight of all those flowers. Everything on it plunged into the baptistry. The candles that had been burning among the flowers were knocked down and they set fire to the red velvet curtains at the sides of the baptistry. At least half a dozen deacons leapt up from various places around the sanctuary, rushed through the side doors to the area behind the chancel, and began shuffling things, pulling down the curtains, and stamping out the fire. Happily, they quickly got it under control.

To its credit, our choir didn't miss a beat. The director kept waving his arms, and we continued singing as if nothing was happening behind us. Not one single voice of panic echoed through the sanctuary. The soloists hit all their notes confidently and precisely. Even in the midst of temporary chaos the story of Jesus' birth went on beautifully and dramatically!

One more picture completes the triptych. It had to do with a children's choir I was rehearsing for a Christmas performance in a large Disciples church in our city. Most of the children's voices were sweet and clear, like the voices of angels. All except Roger's. Roger sang in a loud, distinctive monotone. He was so loud, in fact, that he always managed to overpower the rest of the choir and lead it far, far astray from the notes it should be singing.

What to do? The date of our performance was looming. Would it be wrong to pray for Roger to get a sore throat and be unable to sing? And what if my prayer wasn't answered? At almost the last minute, I had a desperate idea.

"Roger," I said one night at practice in a confidential tone, "I need your help. You know the music better than anybody else, and some of the other children are having trouble remembering the words. I want you to stand over here at the end of the front row where the others can see you and simply mouth the words in pantomime so that if they forget them they can watch your lips and remember. Okay?"

I made it very clear to Roger that he wasn't to make a sound. If he did, that would make it obvious to the congregation that he was telling the others what to sing, and he mustn't do that. He must be absolutely silent and only give them their cues by forming the words clearly and beautifully with his lips.

The night of our performance, Roger was the proudest little choir member I had. He did exactly what I had asked him to do. I saw other children looking in his direction when they felt unsure of any words. They often smiled or winked at him when they did. Even Roger's parents were proud of him that night. "Roger always did have a good memory," his mother told me.

This was many years ago. I don't know what Roger became when he grew up. Maybe he's singing in some renowned chorus somewhere. I rather doubt that. Somehow I can imagine he became a mime!

Christmas is a very serious occasion. But even serious occasions often have some humor about them, and I think the angels in heaven must really enjoy it when the humor breaks through. I have a little portrait known as the Laughing Jesus on my refrigerator. Done originally in charcoal, it is a simple sketch of the familiar face of our Lord, only with his head thrown back and engaged in a hearty, soul-satisfying laugh. I keep it there to remember that even the Savior of the world liked to laugh at things. I think even he would have laughed at some of these things I remember.

Prayer: O God, let us therefore be merry and put sorrow away, for Christ Jesus our Savior was born on this day. Amen.

Stars

When they saw that the star had stopped, they were overwhelmed with joy. —*Matthew 2:10*

Like so many others, I am prone to become over-busy at Christmas. I can't help taking on more tasks than I'm capable of performing. Before I know it, I feel like a hamster on a wheel, going faster and faster, yet getting nowhere. Then I feel frantic and wonder where my Christmas spirit has gone!

I was feeling this way one evening last December when my husband insisted we go out for our long evening walk. It was a crisp, clear night, but not so cold as to be uncomfortable. So we bundled up and trekked along the familiar country roads near our house.

The sky was cloudless and there was no moon. The stars were shining magnificently, as clear as jewels on a velvet background. We stopped to see how many constellations we could identify. As we stared into the heavens, they became alive to me the way they used to when I was a little child. I remembered my mother's saying to me whenever we saw a falling star, "If you can catch it,

Anne, you will always have good luck." She also said that if I wished upon a star, whatever I wished would come true. It all seemed magical to me then, and that night, as I recalled those times, it seemed magical again.

Once in the summertime Mother and I were lying on a quilt in the side yard, waiting for the house to cool off so we could go inside and go to bed. Mother told me that no one had ever made a completely accurate count of all the stars. If I could do that, she said, I would be famous. So, like a little doofus, I began counting them. I counted and counted and counted until at last I fell asleep. The next day I was disappointed because I knew I would have to start over if I was ever going to get an accurate tally.

I thought of these things as my husband and I stood there staring up into the heavens. The memories brought a smile to my face. What a vast and beautiful galaxy we live in, I realized, and how small it renders my little human efforts to make Christmas happen. I could feel my shoulders relaxing and my neck muscles uncramping. Then I remembered the lisping little boy in a church play who loudly proclaimed, when it was his big moment to speak, "A thtar, a thtar, I thaw a thtar!"

Recalling his glorious pronouncement, I looked for the Christmas star. I wasn't sure which one it was, but I thought I found it. When I did, I said, "Isn't it lovely! It puts everything else in perspective."

Prayer: Help me to keep my perspective, O Lord, and not get lost in all the busyness of the season. You didn't send your Son to make my life busier, but to make it easier and more meaningful. Amen.

Lamb

"Here is the Lamb of God." —*John 1:29*

It seems almost ironic, in light of the gospel of John's proclamation that Jesus was the Lamb of God (Jn. 1:29), that the first outsiders to witness the birth of Jesus—that is, those who weren't members of his family—were a group of shepherds who had been keeping watch over their flocks in the nearby Judean hills. "Let us go now to Bethlehem," they said after they had heard the angels' announcement of the birth, "and see this thing that has taken place, which the Lord has made known to us" (Lk. 2:15).

I've sometimes wondered what happened to those men's sheep when they left them to go to Bethlehem and see the Christ child. They must not have been in an enclosure, or the shepherds wouldn't have had to stand watch over them. So did they scatter when the shepherds left and maybe mingle with other shepherds' flocks? Would the shepherds have had to round them up the next day and make sure they were all safe?

Several years ago my husband and I were hiking in the English Lake District. We had a packed lunch with us and found a path winding up a steep hillside to a spot that overlooked a lake and a small town far below. Sheep were grazing all over the hillside. As we climbed toward the summit, they began following us. When we stopped to catch our breath, they stopped. When we talked to them, they cocked their heads and looked at us as if they were trying to understand what we were saying. Each one seemed to have its own personality and was trying to comprehend our presence in its own way.

One sheep was pathetically mangy, unlike its companions, whose fleeces were full and beautiful. "Whatever happened to you?" I asked it in mock sympathy. No sooner had I uttered the words than the sheep seemed to hang its head in embarrassment and sauntered away down the hill. I worried that I had hurt its feelings. Ever since, I have wondered if sheep are as dumb as they're rumored to be. That one, at least, seemed extremely sensitive.

At the peak of the hill a large ewe was in the process of giving birth to a new lamb. As we watched, her eyes seemed to lock onto mine. I felt that she was pleading for help. I began softly talking to her as she struggled to produce the lamb. Then I sang to her. Her gaze never left my face. In a few minutes her little lamb appeared. Instantly the ewe got awkwardly to her feet and began to lick the new baby.

"Good show, girl!" I said to her. But she was too busy now to notice. She had a little lamb to care for.

The shepherds who came to the stable where Jesus was born probably found his mother caring for him in a similar way. We have to wonder if they thought of him as a new little lamb and imagined him as one who would one day grow up to become the Lamb of God whose blood would be shed for the sins of the world.

Whether they did or not, we can't get away from associating Jesus with that image of the Lamb of God. Shepherds through the ages have proudly recalled that it was a few of their number who were first honored with a look at the newborn Savior. For centuries, images of lambs have adorned altars, cathedral windows, the stoles of priests, and anything else symbolizing Christianity. Every Christmas we put a little glass lamb on our tree, a gift from a dear friend, and remember Jesus' association with the sheep. It is one of the rich traditions of the season.

Prayer: Thank you, O God, for this beautiful image of Christ, so pure and innocent and harmless. Help us to conform to that image ourselves, and honor him by being like him. Amen.

Hard Times

Do not be dismayed. —*Jeremiah 46:27*

Bring in the holly and the mistletoe! Hang up the stockings! Trim the tree with colorful lights and ornaments! Set candles in the windows! Christmas time is here again, calling for parties, presents, cookies, candies, punch, and lots of merriment.

But wait a minute. A lot of people don't feel like celebrating. Times have been very hard, and they have lost their fervor for being merry. Many of them probably feel as if life is only an enormous house of horrors where they are forced to suffer and grieve and cannot find the exit.

What would help to restore these poor souls to a sense of the beauty and majesty of the season?

Sometimes when I am feeling weighed down and have trouble getting into the Christmas spirit, I go back and read Truman Capote's *Christmas Memories* again. In that short book the famous author remembers his own childhood during the years of the Great Depression and how he spent most of his time with some elderly female cousins in a small Southern town. Times were hard for almost everybody then, and his cousins didn't have very much.

But Sook, his favorite cousin, didn't let their poverty impede her sense of Christmas magic. Each year she saved her pennies and nickels to buy the ingredients for thirty fruitcakes that she made and distributed to family, friends, and even the occasional distant recipient such as President Franklin Delano Roosevelt. Buddy, as she called young Truman, was always elected to help.

On a crisp, cold morning a few weeks before Christmas, Sook would announce, "It's fruitcake weather, Buddy." They would take their little cache of coins and count them out carefully before going to the store, saving back a few for mailing three or four of the cakes. Then they took an old hand wagon down to the general store and purchased the ingredients they would need. On the way home they would stop at Mr. Ha-Ha Jones's place—he was the resident bootlegger—and buy the bottle of brandy that would flavor the cakes after they came from the oven. When they got back with all their purchases, they would chop the nuts and fruits, stir the batter, taste the batter to be sure it was perfect, and then bake the cakes.

The whole process was a ritual as sacred as the serving of Mass in a great cathedral. Everything was performed in a serious, thoughtful way. Sook and Buddy were as happy sharing their meager resources this way as if they had been priestess and priest at some high altar.

When the cakes had been baked and wrapped, it was time to get a Christmas tree. So the two of them would trudge through the piney woods until they found just the perfect tree for that year. Buddy would cut it down, and they would carry it home and decorate it with the same old treasures they had always used.

That done, they would sing carols and hold hands and dance around the tree, feeling the soft and wondrous glow of Christmas in their hearts.

At the end of his book, Capote tells about one Christmas when he and Sook made one another kites for Christmas gifts. What could have been simpler? Yet they loved those kites, and rejoiced in them as much as if they had been expensive gifts from some elegant department store. On Christmas morning, they could hardly wait to get out in the field and raise those handmade kites aloft, where the currents seized them and bore them high into the wintry sky. They played with them for hours, chasing through the field, tangling their lines, and collapsing on one another in laughter and joy.

Christmas isn't destroyed by hard times. In fact, the very opposite is true. Christmas thrives on hard times!

Jesus wasn't born in a palace. He was born in a stable. He didn't live as a wealthy landowner. He lived as an itinerant preacher. He didn't leave a big estate when he died. He left a simple robe, and those who crucified him cast lots to see who would get it.

Christmas isn't about things at all. It's about love and joy and hope. It's about God putting his arms around us wherever we are, however hard a time we're having, and giving us a sense of his transcendent presence. What could possibly be richer?

Prayer: O God, save us from getting lost in dreams of splendor and help us to rejoice in the Child who was born in a stable far from palaces and plenty, for yours is the only glory that really matters. Amen.

Carols

Sing, O heavens, for the Lord has done it;
    shout, O depths of the earth;
break forth into singing.
    —*Isaiah 44:23*

Since the angels sang of the Messiah's birth, it has
never been possible to separate music from Christmas.
Sometime during the Middle Ages the tradition of
mummers began—people going from door to door at
various times of the year, especially Christmas, staging
little plays and sometimes singing. Probably out of this
sprang up the tradition of caroling, with its emphasis
on going from house to house and singing about the
birth of Christ. With the exception of Ebenezer Scrooge,
almost everybody has loved the singing of the old carols
that celebrate the joy of Christmas. And even he came to
love them!

For several years I was the organist for the tiny
Little Stone Church on Mackinac Island, Michigan,
not far from the Canadian border. The church is
open only seasonally, from May to October, when the
quaint village welcomes an influx of visitors and a few

"cottagers," as they are called. Cottagers own homes and visit the island during the warmer months. Those of us who were actually members of the church didn't see one another at Christmas, but were scattered all over the country. One year we decided we ought to hold a special "Christmas in July," when we could celebrate Christ's coming the way we would if we were together in December. We decorated the church with trees, garlands, and candles. We sang carols, read the Advent scriptures, and had a sermon about the birth of Jesus.

Everyone enjoyed "Christmas in July" so much that we carried on the young tradition for several years.

Ironically, I discovered only recently that the very first recorded singing of carols in America was by the Huron Indians at an Indian mission at Mackinac, Michigan, in 1645. The French priests who first explored the Great Lakes area of our country established a mission school for the Indians on Mackinac Island. Very likely, there, in a little chapel built of hewn trees, bark, and fir branches, the priests taught their Indian converts to sing hymns in honor of the Christ child.

A Jesuit priest named Father Jean de Brebeuf wrote a carol in the Huron language and set it to an old French tune he knew. Sung in the Huron tongue for many years, it was eventually translated into English as "'Twas in the Moon of Wintertime." It told of how "in the moon of wintertime" the birds had all gone south, so God sent angel choirs to take their place. The very stars in the heavens grew dim before their shining, and wondering hunters heard them singing, "Jesus, your King, is born; Jesus is born! In excelsis gloria!"

The tender Babe was found "within a lodge of broken bark," it said, wrapped in a ragged robe of rabbit skins. And as the hunters drew near the lodge, the words sounded out ever more clearly: "Jesus, your King, is born; Jesus is born! In excelsis gloria!"

I have felt very strange about this discovery, thinking what an odd coincidence it is that we had our "Christmas in July" services in a setting that was probably only a few hundred yards from where those Native Americans were singing Christmas carols more than 350 years ago. I like the feeling of connectedness it gives me, of being somehow linked to the past and knowing how Christ was honored centuries earlier in a place I have come to know and love as much as any place in the world.

But isn't that what Christ's birth was about? Didn't it make us one with all our brothers and sisters around the world in every age? What a rich heritage we have in Christ! How wonderful it is to celebrate his birth in our time, building as we do on traditions that go back hundreds and hundreds of years! In excelsis gloria indeed!

Prayer: Help us to be mindful, O God, of the adoration of Christ in hundreds of lands across hundreds of years, and to be grateful for the privilege of joining all the millions of worshipers who have gone before us in the faith. Amen.

Animals

And she gave birth to her firstborn son and wrapped him in bands of cloth, and laid him in a manger. —*Luke 2:7*

A recent TV news program ran a segment about a new airline developed exclusively for animals. Called Pet Jet, the company was formed to provide a safer, more comfortable way for people's pets to travel from one destination to another than the conventional way, which calls for them to be kept in the hold of the plane. When the camera people went inside one of Pet Jet's planes, we saw it had no seats at all for passengers, only some widely spaced shelves for the storing of pet carriers.

"We felt there should be a safe, pleasant way for people to send their pets," said one of the new firm's owners. Apparently many pet-owners agreed, for Pet Jet's flights had all been pre-booked for more than two months in advance, and the company was working hard to expand as rapidly as possible.

Historically people probably haven't always had such high regard for animals. Happily the animals, like women and children, have enjoyed a better status since the coming of Christ.

Sociologists say that women have fared much better since the Middle Ages, when the adoration of Mary, the mother of Jesus, reached its culmination in Europe. The same sociologists say that children have enjoyed more respect because of the writings of the English novelist Charles Dickens, whose own feelings for children were informed by the Christmas story. Similarly, it is thought that the tradition of portraying animals being present at Christ's birth has given them a higher status in the modern world.

Like the author of "The Friendly Beasts" carol, I like to imagine what the animals might have said that evening if they could really have spoken to one another.

Perhaps the donkey said, "It's very late, and I'm awfully weary. Can the rest of you imagine me, with my short little legs, carrying a pregnant woman on my back all the way from Nazareth to Bethlehem? It was a long and difficult trip, even though we rested at night. The pretty lady called Mary was very tired too, but she never complained. I think she was really more concerned about me than she was about herself."

Maybe the cow told how hungry Mary and Joseph were when they arrived at the stable and how happy she had been to give them some milk.

"Well," interrupted the goat, "I had a part in that too. Every day I have given my milk to the innkeeper's wife. She always makes it into cheese. I noticed that the innkeeper brought a plate of that cheese to them shortly after they arrived. They ate heartily of it too."

"Ah," said the sheep in a slow, deliberate voice, "if we're going to talk about the part we've all had in this event, then I must remind you that the blanket the innkeeper loaned the Holy Family was made from the wool I provided last summer. You can see the child wrapped in it now, and it's as soft as a little lamb's wool. I was younger then, you know."

At this, the horse stamped his feet and said, "That's all very well, sheep. But I think we've all helped to provide the warmth for our visitors in this stable. My breath, as it is much greater than yours, has done the most to take the chill off the evening air."

"Hold on there, horse," said the camels, who had put their heads into the stable to eat some of the grain placed there by their masters, the wise men from the East. "We're bigger than you are, and it stands to reason that our breath does more to warm this place than yours. Besides, we're all tired from our long journey and carrying the weight of our masters and the gifts they have brought to the Christ child. Some of these men weigh quite a bit!"

"Listen to you," said the doves in the rafters, "and how you carry on. We've all given something for this special family. We doves gave up some of the straw that would have made our own nests. The little Holy One is asleep on it now. We helped him to go to sleep by cooing softly as his mother rocked him."

Is all of this too fanciful?

Those of us who love "The Friendly Beasts" don't think so.

Prayer: Thank you, God, for the loving-kindness with which you regard all living things—including all the pets and other animals that share this special world with us who are made in your image. Amen.

Celebration

"For you always have the poor with you."
—*Matthew 26:11*

Years ago, when my husband was teaching in a university, our family had the wonderful privilege of spending a year in France, where he was working on a book and served as Theologian-in-Residence for the American Church in Paris. Because of this arrangement, we lived in a lovely apartment in the church building overlooking the River Seine. Our Christmas that year was one of the most enchanting of our lives.

We made many memories in Paris—of lovely little back streets, quaint old shops, marvelous restaurants, great museums, soaring cathedrals, beautiful music, and Christmas scenery we'll never forget. The trees along the Seine were strung with white lights, and when we looked down from our apartment windows, they gave the appearance of a never-ending fairyland.

The services at the American Church were fantastic. The legendary old organist and choir master, Edmond Pendleton, had the great cathedral choir perform one of his own cantatas on Christmas eve. After hearing it, we went with friends to the ancient church of St. Sulpice to hear the ninety–year-old organist Marcel Dupre, who was Pendleton's mentor, play one of his final masses. It was an unforgettable experience!

Of all my memories of that very special Christmas, another stands out even more vividly. It was a Christmas dinner given by the women of the church for the *clochards*, the homeless beggars of Paris.

(A legend tells how they became known as *clochards*. The French word *cloche* means "bell." Some tavern owners took pity on the homeless and allowed them to come into their establishments to sleep after the customers had left for the night. Unable to provide beds, the owners stretched ropes across the main space of the taverns, where the beggars could drape themselves in a leaning position to sleep. In the morning, when the first bells began to ring, the ropes were taken down. The beggars became known as *clochards*, or "bell people.")

At first we worried that the *clochards* might not come to the church. Many lived under bridges along the River Seine. Others were scattered around buildings and alleys from one side of Paris to the other, so we had no easy way to communicate with them. All we could do was send word to a few who lived nearest our church and hope they would spread it to the others.

The night of the dinner, however, they all showed up. Hundreds of them! Most of them were shy about entering a church building. Somehow most of them had managed to clean themselves up far better than usual. When the doors of the church hall were opened, they filed in with solemn dignity and respect. It was obvious that they were astonished at seeing so much food laid out on the tables for them. Once they had sat at the tables and a prayer had been offered, they dug in with a rapacity that was hard to believe. Some probably hadn't eaten so well for years.

A few, in fact, ate too ravenously. Unaccustomed to so much rich food, they gorged themselves—and then had to find their way to the restroom and regurgitate what they had eaten. But then they would come back and eat more cautiously.

Before the evening was over, everyone gathered around the piano to sing carols and share stories. Then, at midnight, a voice that sounded as if it belonged to a radio announcer boomed out in French:

> Gloire à Dieu dans les lieux tres hauts
> Et paix sur la terre parmi les hommes qu'il agrée!
>
> (Glory to God in the highest
> And on earth, peace among men of good will.)

After that, the room fell silent. Finally, each *clochard* said "Glory to God" as he or she went out the door.

I know the Holy Child would have smiled with unaffected pleasure at the radiant light shining from the faces of those humble people who were celebrating his birth that night in one of the world's great cities. I have to smile at it even now as I recollect it.

Prayer: Dear God, let me remember how much the poor mean to you, especially at Christmas time. Amen.

Bells

On that day, there shall be inscribed on the bells of the horses, "Holy to the Lord." —*Zechariah 14:20*

Many years ago the poet Longfellow wrote,

"For bells are the voice of the church;
They have tones that touch and search
The hearts of young and old."

As a teenager, I was the assistant organist of a downtown church where the music committee decided that Christmas carols should be played on the church bells every day at noon for thirty minutes throughout Advent. As we didn't have a carillon, the bells were attached to the organ. This meant that someone had to be there to play the organ each day. The regular organist had a job and couldn't be at the church at noon, so I was asked to play the bells.

Although I'm ashamed to admit it now, I resented the assignment. It consumed almost the entirety of my lunch hour to walk to the church, play the bells, and walk back to school. During Christmas vacation, I had a job at the dime store, and it meant losing an hour of work to play the church bells.

When I began playing the carols, I questioned whether anybody even listened to the music of the bells. Most people, I imagined, would be too busy shopping or having lunch at the drugstore to pay much heed to them. So when one day brought a deep snowfall, I was happy to think I would be relieved of playing that day. I would simply say I couldn't get to the church.

My mother, though, had other ideas. She insisted that I don my overshoes and coat and trudge through the snow to the church. "It's your responsibility," she said, "and you can't shirk it just because it's snowing." So, grousing under my breath, I pulled on my overshoes and coat, wrapped a scarf around my head, and trekked off through the snow. Little did I know what I was about to experience.

As I played that day, I kept hearing the church doors creaking open and shut. When the time was finally up, I turned off the organ, stepped away from it, and started gathering my things to leave. Aware of some motion, I looked out into the sanctuary and saw a number of people sitting in the pews. Many were smiling and waving to me.

As I wiggled into my coat, a nearby voice said, "Do you really have to quit? My mother is a shut-in and listens to the bells every day. She came to this country as a girl and says they remind her of the ones she heard as a child in England. They're such a comfort to her. They really make her think of Christmas."

Others began sharing similar stories about how much the bells meant to them or others in their families.

Some spoke of relatives on sick beds. Others of children who delighted in the bells. And still others of how much it lifted the spirits of people in the nearby stores.

Suddenly I was ashamed of myself. I realized how selfish I had been. My playing had been a real ministry to others, and I hadn't known it. From that day until Christmas I played with a totally different attitude. I thought of my playing as an offering to God. Ever since, I have often thought of the line from "Carol of the Bells" that says, "Hark, how the bells send their joyful tone to every home!"

God was using my playing to bless the lives of many people in our community, and I didn't even know it!

Prayer: Lord, help me to think of others during this Christmas season and not of myself. It is the least I can do to thank you for all your gifts to me. Amen.

Mystery

Now we see in a mirror, dimly, but then we will see face to face. —*1 Corinthians 13:12*

One of the things I love about Christmas is its sense of mystery. I like most mysteries—Agatha Christie novels, whodunnit stage plays, and even odd things that happen for which we don't know the explanation. My mind is intrigued by puzzles, by trying to fit things together and understand why they have turned out as they did.

Life itself is a mystery. I often wonder why some people suffer and others don't, why some marriages turn out beautifully and others become like hell on earth, why one business flourishes and another fails, why I feel better on some days than I do on others. I'm sure if I were a good enough analyst, I could come up with the answers to all these questions. But most of the time I simply have to accept things as they are. I may wonder about them, but I won't ever solve the mystery of them.

Even the birth of Jesus was shrouded in mystery. Why did Joseph and Mary have to go to Bethlehem at precisely that time to register and pay their taxes? Why was the Lord of the universe born in a cattle stall? Why did the angels choose to serenade those particular shepherds and tell them about the birth of Christ? Why did the wise men from the East go to see Herod before following their star to the birthplace? Why was Herod so upset about the birth of Jesus? Why was it necessary for Joseph to take his family to Egypt? Couldn't they have hidden as well in some more convenient location?

Many things about Jesus' life remain a mystery. We know very little about his years before he undertook his public ministry, only that he "increased in wisdom and in years, and in divine and human favor" (Lk. 2:52). We know little about his personal life even after that. Was he ever married? Most rabbis were. Did he really work as a carpenter, or was it merely assumed that he did because that was Joseph's trade? What did he look like? The only portraits we have were painted long after he died. Did he always know he would be crucified, or did he have visions of himself as an old man living by the seashore and talking to visitors who came to see him?

Paul was right: now, in this life, we only see things as if we were witnessing them in a dingy, old-fashioned mirror—dim, sketchy, remote, far from clear and easy to understand. We are fated to live with mystery until the time comes when we are with God and can see everything "face to face," directly and totally comprehensible.

We have a number of facts to go on. Mary gave birth to the Savior in Bethlehem, some shepherds came to see him, and so did some wise men (we don't know exactly how many) from the East. From there it is all conjecture and imagination. That's why artists appear to love the birth of Christ—they feel free to interpret it and embellish on it to their hearts' content. We must be content with the summation in the gospel of John: "And the Word became flesh and lived among us, and we have seen his glory, the glory as of a father's only son, full of grace and truth" (Jn. 1:14). In the end, that is the best—and perhaps the most—that can be said.

But I still love a mystery and enjoy my little reveries about the mysteries of Christ's birth as I sit before our glowing Christmas tree and look at the crèche scene beneath it. Maybe it is all too big and too important to resolve in a simple way. Maybe the mystery is important as a cloak for what God was doing in Christ, and I'm not supposed to understand it until I see him face to face. I'm glad I'll know then, but for now, I'll enjoy wondering about it.

Prayer: Thank you, God, for the mystery around Christ's birth and life and death and resurrection. If I could understand it all, it would be too small to be truly meaningful and effective. Amen.

Poinsettias

He [Solomon's craftsman] carved cherubim, palm trees, and open flowers, overlaying them with gold.
—*1 Kings 6:35*

My favorite of all the beautiful flowers and greenery used for decorations at Christmas is the poinsettia. Its brilliant red color lends itself naturally to the excitement of the holidays. When I walk into a church whose chancel is aflame with banks of those gorgeous flowers, my heart seems to skip a beat or two. I want to stand for a moment just basking in the loveliness.

I can almost feel the same emotion when I come upon great crowds of poinsettias in a supermarket or a shopping mall. Wordsworth loved his hosts of teeming daffodils. I'll take displays of poinsettias any time.

When my husband took a pastorate in Los Angeles several years ago, I was delighted to walk into our parsonage and look out the windows upon giant poinsettias growing around our patio. They weren't like the "big" ones I'd seen in florist shops and grocery stores, the ones standing two or three feet high. Some of these were eight or ten feet tall! And the best part was that they bloomed all year, not just at Christmas. I felt as if we lived with a 365–day-a-year miracle right in our own backyard!

Inasmuch as we had poinsettias growing in our yard, I felt it incumbent on me to learn more about those beautiful flowering plants. A little research revealed that they were named for Dr. Joel Roberts Poinsett, a U.S. ambassador to Mexico, who had found them in that country in the mid-nineteenth century. The Mexicans called poinsettias the "flowers of the Holy Night," as they associated their deep red tones with the blood of Christ and hence with the birth of the child who as a man would give his life for the sins of the world.

I also found several legends that had grown up around the poinsettia. My favorite featured two Mexican children, Pablo and Maria, who were brother and sister. Like all the children in their village, they were excitedly looking forward to the setting up of the nativity scene in their church. It was the custom for all the children to bring gifts on Christmas Eve to present to the baby Jesus in the crèche. Unfortunately Pablo and Maria were so poor they didn't even have a few coins with which to buy a gift for the baby.

As they walked to church that night, they searched the roadsides for even a single blossom to bring to the Christ child, but there were none to be seen. In desperation, they plucked a handful of weeds and came to church bearing those. The other children made fun of them, but Pablo and Maria steadfastly approached the manger and laid their pitiful little weeds with the other offerings around the baby.

Suddenly a miracle occurred! The common weeds were transformed into beautiful flowers with bright-red, star-shaped blossoms. Everybody gasped in awe, for they were the most beautiful gift the Christ child received. Ever after that, poinsettias grew throughout Mexico's countrysides as a reminder of the night of Christ's nativity.

I cherish that story, because I have often felt that I had nothing more than weeds to give to Christ along my life's journey. Perhaps, though, in the aura of miracle and surprise that always surrounds him, my gifts too have been transformed into more than I expected. It is comforting to think that that might be the case.

Prayer: I have given you so little, O God, and yet you have blessed me with so much. Forgive the inadequacy of my offerings, and help me to trust that in your grace and generosity they have been accepted. Amen.

Jealousy

We appeal to you, brothers and sisters...Be at peace among yourselves. —*1 Thessalonians 5:12–14*

This may seem like an awful topic to bring up at Christmas time. Jealousy was always considered one of the seven deadly sins, and with good reason. Somehow it manages to corrupt almost any human situation.

Why did King Herod feel that he had to rid himself of Christ, when Christ might have brought a whole new life to the corrupt old monarch? Probably because he couldn't stand the thought of changing. He was the ruler. Why should he pay deference to a child born in a stable in one of his smaller outposts? He was accustomed to people glorifying him. Why should he even think about glorifying a baby? So he behaved in his old, predictable way. Instead of accepting God's gift to the world and humbling himself before the Lord, he set out to kill the child.

Thus jealousy, unpleasant a thought as it is, ensconced itself among the Christmas legends, and a sixteenth-century English carol would tell the story:

Herod, the king,
In his raging,
Charged he hath this day
His men of might,
In his own sight,
All young children to slay.

We easily, almost naturally, become jealous of those who have more than we have—more possessions, more power, more adoration, more beauty, more attention.

A few years ago a dear friend admitted to me that she had spent many years since our graduation from high school being jealous of me. I couldn't understand this, because I didn't think I had anything of which she could possibly be envious.

"You didn't ask me to be in your wedding," she said.

I thought back to my wedding. I had asked two very close friends since first grade to be my attendants, plus another who was coming from a long distance to stand with them. I had asked three friends from our high school class to sing at the wedding, so they too were dressed in pretty organdy dresses and stood in front of the congregation. It had never occurred to me that this particular friend might be hurt or jealous because she wasn't asked to participate.

Now, years later, I was able to understand a little better why this friend had sometimes said or done things that struck me as peculiar or even slightly hostile. I had given her an occasion to be jealous of my other friends who were invited to be part of the wedding. This made me very sad and depressed. How easily people get their feelings hurt. How easily they succumb to jealousy.

Jealousy often ruins people's lives. Families are disrupted and torn apart because one child thinks another got more attention or received more than his or her share of an inheritance. Children's friendships are poisoned because one envies another's new frock or new bicycle, or because he or she got a part in the school play and the other didn't. Even countries become unhappy and sometimes go to war because one resents the other's prosperity or status among the nations.

How sad it all is!

Maybe this is why the story of King Herod's jealousy and obsession about finding and killing all the male children under two years of age found its way into the gospel accounts of Jesus' birth. It was to remind us, even during our celebration of the coming of God's great Light into the world, of the darkness many human beings still harbor in their hearts. What did John the Evangelist say? "He came to what was his own, and his own people did not accept him" (Jn. 1:11).

Jealousy is a dark subject. It would be human to want to forget it in the midst of our celebrations. But the gospel writers obviously wanted us to bear it in mind at all times and be wary lest we ourselves fall into jealousy. Maybe we can start by refusing to be jealous of other people's Christmas decorations or the beautiful clothes they wear to a party or the things they get for presents on Christmas day. That's one way of saying no to Herod and yes to Christ, and letting the glorious Light of Christmas shine in our hearts forever.

Prayer: Help me to guard myself from jealous thoughts and feelings, O God, and instead give glory and honor to the child who was born in Bethlehem's stable all those years ago. Amen.

Old Age

"Master, now you are dismissing your servant in peace." —*Luke 2:29*

Maybe it's because I myself am growing older, but I am often haunted by one part of the Christmas story. Mary and Joseph take the baby Jesus to the temple to fulfill the law about offering a sacrifice for a newborn. Two elderly people encounter them there. Simeon and Anna apparently spent all their time in the temple in prayer. The picture of those two elderly people gazing upon the Holy Child's face and blessing God for having been permitted to see him—the very old looking upon the very young—is classic. How often are older people enraptured at seeing the newborn because the newborn gives them joy and hope for the future!

Only the other night, my husband and I were having dinner with friends in a restaurant. We saw an older couple who had brought their two little grandchildren to dinner, probably to give the parents a night out. It was a beautiful sight, the way the grandparents listened to the children and talked so lovingly to them. We couldn't help smiling as we watched. It was easy to see that those dear children were part of their grandparents' contentment with life and happiness about their own later years. Somehow it made everything worthwhile for them.

Don't you imagine this is what Luke was trying to convey by showing us the portraits of Simeon and Anna beaming at the Holy Child in the temple? Luke was a doctor and had obviously seen a lot of life, so he was sensitive to the feelings of the old and the promise of the young. Simeon was obviously a man of prayer, for God had revealed to him that he would not die before he had laid eyes on God's Messiah. Anna, too, was a person of prayer and devotion. At eighty-four—a great age in those days!—she spent all her time in the temple worshiping God. When she saw the Christ child, she began immediately "to praise God and speak about the child to all who were looking for the redemption of Jerusalem" (Lk. 2:38).

Those two elderly persons were ecstatic to see that God was at last fulfilling his promise to send the Messiah who would save his people. They probably had no idea how grand God's design really was, or how the little child they were seeing would one day grow up to become the center of a worldwide community of faith and love. They did know the baby in their arms was very special and that they were extraordinarily privileged to be able to see him. They both felt as Simeon said he did, that he was then ready to depart in peace, having seen the blessing of God.

I have a lot of elderly friends I'm thinking about this Christmas. Some have lost their mates in the past year. Others are dealing with various physical problems, everything from broken bones and the loss of eyesight to lymphoma and cervical cancer. Whoever said that old age isn't for sissies knew what he or she was talking about. It takes a lot of courage and a lot of stamina to grow older gracefully. I'm thinking about my friends now, and giving thanks that they will all be worshiping the Christ child as I shall. Together, we all have confidence that God has come among us in the Holy Child, Jesus, to point the way to our own salvation. I find that very comforting, for them as well as for myself. I'm glad Luke included this beautiful picture in his gospel, of two old folks chucking little Jesus under his chin and praising God for letting them see him. It's one of the most beautifully human pictures in the Bible!

Prayer: Thank you, God, for the security we feel in Jesus as we grow older. Grant that all my old friends will find joy in him this Christmas. Amen.

Anxiety

"Therefore I tell you, do not worry about your life."
—*Matthew 6:25*

I grew up in a home where anxiety simply abounded. It was understandable, I think. My parents had seven children, one of whom, a little girl, died when she was only a few months old. My father didn't make much money, and things were always tight for us. We lived in a small house and kept chickens and a cow to make ends meet. My four brothers were called into military service during World War Two and fought in Europe and the Far East. They rarely ever wrote home. If they did, their letters didn't reach us. No wonder my parents were anxious and unsettled a lot of the time!

I couldn't say that their anxiety levels were ever raised by having to prepare for Christmas. They didn't seem to care about Christmas or go to any lengths to celebrate it. During the years while my brothers were away, they didn't bother putting up a Christmas tree or hanging a wreath. We never had anything special for Christmas dinner. The only presents we children received were an orange and a candy cane in the stockings we hung by the chimney. My mother and father never gave presents to one another. I have always suspected that it was their lack of enthusiasm for Christmas that made me want to celebrate it so lavishly once I married and left home.

My husband and I have never had cause to be anxious the way my parents were. Yet I have to admit that my anxiety level is raised by all the preparations for Christmas. Maybe I only swapped their kind of anxieties for my own, most of which have to do with seeing that everything is done as perfectly and thoughtfully as possible to make Christmas a wonderful experience each year.

I invariably tend to overdecorate. My husband teases that he can't sit or stand in one place very long or I will festoon him with lights and garlands. I have always shopped and shopped to find just the right presents for the loved ones on my list. I have cleaned the house from stem to stern. Always fastidious about having a spotless house, I am super-fastidious for the holidays. And cooking! I am almost ashamed to say how much effort I put into making cakes and candies and planning menus for extra special meals throughout the season. I really need someone to knock me in the head and say, "That's enough! In fact, that's too much. It's time to stop all this bustling around and enjoy the holidays."

This year I am trying to scale back and thereby reduce my anxieties about Christmas. I have resolved not to spend so many hours getting all the decorations just right or the presents bought or the menus planned. I want to listen to Jesus' words, "Do not worry," and truly heed them. I know I will have a richer, happier Christmas if I can do it.

Instead of dealing with my own anxieties, I want to focus on the anxieties Mary and Joseph must have felt that first Christmas when they were so far from home. How frightened they must have been to leave their home in Nazareth and travel all the way to Bethlehem to enroll and pay their taxes as required by law. How tiring the trip must have been for Mary, and how anxious Joseph must have been about her when she started having labor pains. How that anxiety must have doubled and tripled as he searched for a place to spend the night and found nothing but the stable of an innkeeper. Those were real anxieties. They were problems to be considered and dealt with. There was nothing empty or imaginary about them.

Yet in the midst of whatever anxieties the holy couple experienced, a wondrous calm must have enveloped them when the child was born and angels attended his birth. How did they feel when those motley shepherds showed up at the stable saying they had been led there by angels? And when magi from the Orient said they had followed an unusual star to find the Holy One in the manger?

I can only hope that my own anxieties will be overcome this Christmas by a similar feeling of being caught up in the eternal designs of a loving God. I plan to have a cup of tea, relax, and remember: "For unto us a child is born, unto us a son is given: and the government shall be upon his shoulders, and his name shall be called Wonderful, Counsellor, the Mighty God, the everlasting Father, the Prince of Peace" (Isa. 9:6, Handel's wording).

Prayer: We live in a deeply troubled world, O God. Please help us this Christmas to remember the child who was born to be the Prince of Peace, and let the serenity of his heart be in ours as well. For his name's sake. Amen.

Angels

"He will command his angels concerning you, to protect you."—*Luke 4:10*

How does the old carol go?

Angels from the realms of glory,
Wing your flight o'er all the earth;
Ye, who sang creation's story,
Now proclaim Messiah's birth!

Only a moment's thought about angels gives me a feeling of comfort. Whenever I read the words, "Fear not, for I bring you good tidings," all the heavy burdens are suddenly lifted from my heart, my shoulders go back, and I feel a glorious release from the weight I was carrying.

I am so grateful that angels had such a significant role in the story of Christ's birth and that so many Christmas cards we receive have pictures of angels on them. Some of the angels appear tall and regal; others are plump and jolly. But they are all reminders of a transcendent reality that lies everywhere about us, whether we live in awareness of it or not. If we don't live with great sensitivity to their presence, the fault is ours, not theirs, for they are always present, ready to do God's bidding.

When my sister's husband died a few years ago, she told me her house felt empty without him. For several weeks she didn't sleep well at night because she was afraid to be alone. My husband and I lived several states away and couldn't go to be with her during this time of anxiety. So I sent her a little terra cotta angel I found in a gift store and asked her to set it on the table by her bed.

"If you feel afraid," I said, "pick up this angel and hold it. It is going to be your guardian angel now that you don't have Henry there to help you."

She told me that she often did this and that the angel gave her comfort. It reminded her that she wasn't alone because God's real guardian angel was there with her too.

I wasn't just trying to make her feel safe. I really believe in guardian angels.

A few years ago my husband had lung surgery to remove a strange little spot the doctors couldn't diagnose without looking at it. The operation went well, and he was on the road to recovery when, a few days later, he dropped a pillow in his hospital room and bent over to pick it up. Wham! His heart and lungs were suddenly attacked by a barrage of embolisms. He couldn't get his breath. Fortunately, a young doctor we had met a few days earlier was sitting in his room when this happened and immediately started procedures to take care of the problem.

Because his situation was so precarious—the doctors gave him only a 40 percent chance of surviving—he had to be kept in ICU. Hospital personnel told me to go on back to my hotel room for the night.

Our son and his wife were with me. As we were leaving the hospital, we passed a small chapel and went in to have prayer. The Roman Catholic hospital had a beautiful wooden reredos or ornamental screen at the front of the chapel with carvings of the Way of the Cross on it. We knelt and commenced to pray. After a while I became very weary and eased myself back onto the pew. Our son moved back at the same time.

I was staring at the reredos when a strange thing happened. Something white and wraithlike emerged from the reredos—right out of the beautiful wood—and drifted past us, up the aisle, and out the back door. I thought I was hallucinating. But when I noticed that my son's eyes were open too, I asked him, "Did you see something?"

"Yes," he said.

"What was it?"

"It was something white. It came from the chancel and went past us up the aisle." His tone was very serious. "Do you think it was the Angel of Death?"

"No," I said. "It was white. It must be your dad's guardian angel."

In that moment, I knew that my husband would be all right. I had never had such an experience before, and I have not had one since. But seeing that "angel" was one of the truest, most real things that ever happened to me. And it is important to me that I wasn't the only one who saw it. Our son, who is a psychologist, had seen it too. Later he wrote a paper about the experience.

"Fall on your knees," says the carol, "and hear the angels' voices!"

That's a good idea. They are, after all, sent from God.

Prayer: Help us, dear Lord, in this busy and unbelieving world, to hear the voices and pay attention to the leading of your messengers. For your name's sake. Amen.

Home

When they had finished everything required by the law of the Lord, they returned to Galilee, to their own town of Nazareth. —*Luke 2:39*

"Home is where the heart is." That old saying is never more true than during the Christmas holidays, when everybody longs to go home. A great migration spreads out all over the country as people take to the highways, trains, and airplanes to get back to their places of origin and celebrate the birth of Christ in old familiar places. The words of the popular song, "I'll be home for Christmas, you can plan on me," are part of our psyche. They can bring tears to the eyes of anybody who can't make it home.

My husband and I have always wanted to be home at Christmas. When we were first married, we went to visit our parents over the holidays. As our children came along, we made it a rule to have Christmas in our own home first, then go to visit their grandparents. After our children left home, we established the practice of always being at home for Christmas even if no one else was able to come, because it gave us strength and comfort to know that we were going to celebrate with our own tree, our own Christmas music, and our own fire on the hearth.

All this seems a little ironic when we consider that Jesus and his parents were away from home when he was born. Joseph, being descended from King David, was compelled by a government edict to travel with his young wife, Mary, to Bethlehem, the town associated with David, to be registered and taxed by the Roman officials there. As the story goes, "While they were there, the time came for her to deliver her child" (Lk. 2:6). Irony upon irony, when the time came for Mary to have her baby, there was no room in anybody's home for them. So this homeless man and woman repaired to a stable, where she gave birth to the Savior of the world and laid him in a manger.

The ancient churchman Augustine once said, "Thou hast made us for thyself, and our hearts are restless until they rest in Thee." Maybe the Holy Family's own homelessness at the time of Jesus' birth was a symbol of the human condition. We always have a kind of homelessness in us until we find our way to God. And our Lord, according to the apostles John and Paul, left his heavenly home to wander among us as an itinerant Savior until we find our way through him to the Father.

I want to think about that this Christmas. Maybe even more important than being home for Christmas is being at home in God for Christmas. I have to contemplate that and ask myself, "Are you really home? Is your heart resting in God?"

Anthropologist Loren Eiseley tells in *All the Strange Hours*[1] how homesick he became as a young man living out West for his health. During the Great Depression he had no money to go home, so he did what many people did, he stole a ride on a freight train going east. But the top of the car he attempted to mount was so crowded that he had to ride hanging onto the iron ladder on its side. Tired of traveling and longing for sleep, he hung on for dear life, knowing he would probably die if he fell. The train rumbled through the night and eventually stopped for refueling in Kansas City.

Eiseley knew he had been asleep, but his arms had held fast to the ladder. He dropped stiffly to the ground. A night watchman approached. "Where are we?" asked the weary boy. "Kansas City," said the watchman. Then the watchman said, "You ought to be careful, son. You could kill yourself, you know." Almost as an afterthought, he asked, "Where you goin' in such a hurry?"

The young man thought with horror that the watchman was right. He could have been killed that night if he had fallen from the ladder.

"I'm going home," he said.

I resonate to that story. And I think how desperately I want to be at home in God this Christmas.

Prayer: It's Christmas, O God, and I want to be at home in you. Help me to find my way through Jesus, who was born on this day! Amen.

---

[1]New York: Scribner, 1975.

The Tax Collector:
A Christmas Monologue

by John Killinger

You want to talk to me? That was a long time ago. My memory may not be entirely accurate. But I suppose you're right. There aren't many who can remember it all. My faulty memory may be better than none.

I was a tax collector. One of Caesar's men. God knows, I wasn't very old. Maybe twenty or twenty-one, I can't remember. My father, bless his soul, got me the appointment. He had done a favor for the governor, and the governor wanted to reward him. Papa said no, but the governor insisted. So Papa said, "Well, I've got a boy. Maybe you could do something for him."

Before I knew it, I was packed off to Bethlehem, which wasn't much more than a wide spot in the road. They made me the official tax collector for the area. I was still a boy, mind you, and not an inch taller than I am today! *(Laughs)*

Well, maybe an inch. But I was still quite small.

I hadn't been there more than a month or two when word came down from Rome that they were going to reconstruct the whole tax roll. Imagine that! There I was, greener than an avocado, and suddenly my little office got the biggest assignment it had ever had. *(Chuckles)* It's a wonder I didn't throw up my hands and run.

We registered something over eight thousand people in the next six months. Made a record of who they were, where they were living—they had to return to their hometowns to register, you understand—whether they were married and had children, what they owned, how old they were, whether they'd ever served in the military, all the things like that.

It was a big job, the biggest of my lifetime. And money! You wouldn't believe all the money we handled in those six months. People had to pay their taxes when they registered, you see. I had two soldiers, members of the twenty-second legion, stationed outside my office the whole time. Even when the office was closed, guards stayed there to make sure no one stole the money. It was something else, I'll tell you.

Oh yes, I remember. That fellow Joseph, from up north. A carpenter. He was a carpenter. Came all the way down from Caesarea or Nazareth or some such place. And his wife. She was a pretty, young thing. Didn't look a day over fifteen or sixteen, as I remember. But pregnant as a skin full of wine! I mean, she looked as if she were ready to deliver at any minute. I was worried she might have the baby right there on my fine carpet. Such a sweet face! Not like a lot of these modern girls with their fancy, highflown ways. You could tell she was a good country lass with old-fashioned values. It was written all over her and the way she smiled at her husband.

Well, now, Joseph—he was a lot older than she was, which didn't make a lot of difference to me—Joseph gave us all the information we were required to take, and counted out the money he owed us—the government, that is—and then he asked if I knew any place where he and his young woman could spend the night. He said he'd stopped at every inn along the way into Bethlehem, and they were already full. In fact, the whole town was full, had been for days. A lot of folks were visiting their kin, inasmuch as they had to be there anyway, so there wasn't even a private home I could recommend to him. The house where I roomed had been taken over by more of the landlord's relatives than I'd ever seen under one roof. I had two old geezers sharing my bed, which made me right uncomfortable, I can tell you. Especially as they weren't relatives of mine.

To tell you the truth, I don't know why I paid any attention to their situation. Plenty of folks were in the same boat they were in. I guess it was that pretty young wife of his who smiled at me as gentle as if I'd brought her a dipper of cool milk. I couldn't see her left to spend the night in a field. Not in the condition she was in. So I said why didn't they come down the road to where I lived—it was only a short way out of town—and put up in the little shed behind the house.

You'd have thought I handed them the moon, the way they thanked me. They waited as patient as stones out in the street until I closed the office an hour or so later. Then they went along with me.

He was a fine-looking man, Joseph was. Strong and bronzed, with a pair of hands that could have choked a mountain lion! I think he gave his age as fifty when I registered him. She was only seventeen. I worried about her walking the distance to where I lived, but she only smiled. Joseph said not to be concerned, she was strong and healthy.

Well, by the time we got there, two more people were already in the shed, but Joseph said it didn't matter. They were happy to find a corner of the place with some clean straw. They would travel on the next day and try to find something a little closer to Jerusalem.

(A slight pause, as if marveling at the memory)

Golly, it was something! I had no idea what was about to happen in that little shed. Nobody did, I guess. It was just one of those...*(Pauses, gets a little choked up)* Sorry. I sometimes get a little teary-eyed thinking about it. Who would have guessed? That young girl, who had traveled all that distance with a child inside her, the mother of...*(Chokes up)* Excuse me...*(Sniffs, clears his throat)*

I ate my dinner, same as always, though about three times as many people as usual crowded around the table that night. I was sitting there listening to the tales being told by some of the relatives—one was a real talker!—when I remembered Joseph and the girl. I knew they probably had some stuff with them, but I wasn't sure if they had any food. So I asked the landlord's wife if I could take a plate out to them. I ladled out some of the stew she'd fixed and put a couple of pieces of bread on it and carried it out to the shed.

They were alone out there now, their stable companions being relatives inside at the table. They seemed real pleased I had brought them something. Joseph offered to pay for it, but I wouldn't take it. I said it wouldn't be hospitable to accept anything. He thanked me heartily. Her eyes looked at me as gratefully as if I'd brought them a seven-course meal.

Joseph asked if it'd be all right if he filled their waterbag from the well beside the house.

I said sure, I'd go with him, as I'd brought a lantern from the house. He kept saying how grateful they were for a place to spend the night and for the food. I hadn't done a lot of kind deeds in my life, as I was still very young. I was feeling pretty good about myself.

Glad I could be of help, I said, and lit the way back to the shed.

We heard her moaning before we'd reached the door.

"Mary!" he said. "What's the matter? Are you all right?"

"I'm—I'm—It's the baby," she said. "I think he's coming!"

I remember at the time thinking it was funny she said "he," as if she already knew it would be a boy.

Oh yes, he was coming, right as rain. It didn't take any time, as such things go. My wife's firstborn was eleven hours from when the first real pains hit. But that baby didn't waste any time. I barely had time to fetch the landlord's wife, who had three of her own and knew something about such matters, before that girl was perspiring and crying and heaving like a wrestler trying to get his breath after a hard blow to the stomach. Oh, it was something, I tell you! It was something! That baby knew when it was time to come, and he didn't wait for an engraved invitation.

(Looks up) What? Oh, excuse me a moment. I promised this man something. It won't take a minute.

(Walks to side of stage, gestures as if talking with someone, comes back to center)

There, that was quick enough, wasn't it?

Where was I? Oh yes. Mary was having her baby, right there in the corner of the shed. There wasn't any other way for it. She was having it, and that was all there was to it. Joseph, he was as helpless as a bed sheet in a windstorm. He was so nervous he just kept getting in the way. Finally, the landlord's wife sent him out for more water just to get rid of him. I guess I wasn't much better. I'd never seen a baby born before, and I didn't have a clue about what to do. I just sort of stood there, and stooped down and held a cool cloth to Mary's forehead when the landlord's wife told me to. Mary held onto my arm when the contractions got too bad and she needed to hold on to something.

Nature and the good Lord did the rest, I suppose, as they always do. It couldn't have been twenty minutes, thirty at the most, before she delivered. She was panting hard and moaning. Then she gave this one sharp little scream, and there he was. His head, at least. Then the rest of him. Just like that, slick as a ribbon! Little red face, his eyes closed tight, his little hands reaching out like they wanted to grab the air itself, his legs twitching and kicking.

"What're you going to call him?" I asked Joseph when he got back with the water.

"Joshua," his wife said. "His name will be Joshua."

That's Jesus, you know, in the Roman world. But she used the old Hebrew name.

People ask me, "Did he cry?"

No, not a sound. Just his hands and his feet moving, and his mouth screwed up a little, like he wanted to say something but couldn't. Not yet, anyway. Suddenly his eyelids parted. Those great brown eyes looked out at everything—the cow and the donkey and the goats and the landlord's wife and me—I had the feeling he was looking right at me—and right through me, at the same time. I hadn't ever seen a baby born before, but I've seen several since—four of my own—and I've never seen a newborn baby so alert, so fully aware, so, well, almost in command of things.

He never did cry. The landlord's wife cleaned him off and handed him to his mama. She put him up to her breast, and he began sucking as calmly as if he'd been at the dinner pail before and knew exactly what to do. There wasn't any screaming or any hysterics or anything. He just came into the world as if it was his and that was what he was supposed to do. When I think back on it, it was—well, sort of awesome.

(Glances to side of stage as if hearing something)

Oh, excuse me again. That child needs something I have. I'll be right back.

(Walks to side of stage, again converses with someone unseen, and returns)

I told her if she'd come around I'd have it for her. There. She's all fixed up now. We shouldn't be interrupted again.

Yessir, it was awesome.

What? Those sheepherders? Yes, I'm getting around to that part. I wasn't going to leave it out.

Well, you see, I went back to my room after things quieted down. The landlord's wife said they didn't need us intruding on their privacy, so we returned to the house. I couldn't sleep, not with those two fellows wheezing and snoring in my room. I tossed and turned for a while. Finally, I got up and eased out to the shed to make sure everything was all right. I noticed this strange light out there. I mean, the barnyard was lit up like a star was hovering over it. The hayrick and the eaves and the shed door standing open all cast shadows the way they do at noontime. I didn't know what was happening.

Then I began hearing this—this—unearthly music! I thought I was hallucinating! I told myself I was having a dream. It had to be a dream, because of the light and the music and everything. It was wonderful! I felt as if I just might start flying around the house or something, it was so dreamlike.

I looked in the door, figuring I'd be very quiet and not disturb anybody. Lo and behold, a bunch of fellows was in there, all crowded around Mary and Joseph and little Joshua. Rough fellows, all of them. I could see that. But they were being as gentle as if it was their own baby that had just been born, all speaking softly and cooing to him, sticking out their grubby fingers for him to hold onto. It was a night of miracles, and they were all a part of it.

I'd never seen a sight like it, and I haven't since. Those grungy old fellows—not all of them were old, some were younger than I was—behaving like a bunch of silly billies over that baby!

Mind you, I thought he was pretty special too. It was clear to me by this time, with that eerie light and strange music, and then those shepherd fellows there out of nowhere, that something very unusual was happening. I didn't know fully what it was—not then. I hadn't put God's name to it yet, but I was starting to suspect. Suddenly I could hear words in the music—the most beautiful voices—and they were singing, "Glory to God in the highest!"

I knew then.

I'd never dreamed it would happen, but I knew that something very special and unusual was happening there that night. I was caught up in it, the way a sheep gets caught up in the shearing. I couldn't get out of it if I wanted to. Of course, I didn't want to get out of it. I never did, but especially not now, now that I realized this had to be God's own Messiah that was born there, right in that, that stable, and that I had had a part in seeing him born. I still get goosebumps thinking about it. Imagine! Being in on his coming into the world! It's bound to change everything—your whole life.

(Hears something again)

What? Oh, excuse me again. Someone else I need to see. Just a moment. I won't be long. This fellow's in real need. I know him.

(Walks to side of stage, then returns)

Sorry.

I expect you'll want to hear about those princes from the East. Most people do. Wise men, some said. Wealthy men, at any rate, and connected with royalty. That's what they said, the ones who saw them.

I wasn't there myself. We had finished the registration a couple of days earlier, and I rode along with the records and the money to deliver them to the governor up in Antioch. I heard plenty when I got back, all about their strange garb and their fancy gear and the unusual languages they spoke. And the gifts they brought! Oh, I saw those, all right. A cask of gold coins worth a king's ransom! And furs! Mary tried to give me one for my bed, but I said it was too rich for me. And exotic containers of strange perfumes! One of them, when she opened it, made me think of foreign spices and citrus groves and warm summer nights, all rolled together.

They said a star had led them there. Imagine following a star hundreds and hundreds of miles, maybe thousands, and all at night, across dark rivers and unknown landscapes. Yes, I suppose you could call that faith. I don't think any of us could really brag about having a lot of faith. It just happened to us. Now if there hadn't been a light, or any heavenly music, and we had still understood—that might have been faith. But I'm not a rabbi. These things are too deep for me.

What's that? Didn't I live a life of faith? No, I can't really say I did. You know how it is. You have a great experience, and you think you understand it, but you don't really grasp the significance at the time. Before you know it, you've slipped back into the usual pattern of things, and it all sort of gets away from you.

Yes, that's what happened to me. I had done a good job with the registration in Bethlehem, and my father did another good turn for the governor. Before I knew it, I had been appointed to a much bigger office here in Jericho—one of the biggest in the region, as a matter of fact. I was soon caught up in my work. I got married and built a big house—no, not this one, one several times larger than this—and had a lot of servants. Then we had children. One thing led to another. Life just got out of hand, the way it does for a lot of people, and I seldom thought about what I had witnessed that night. I'm ashamed to admit it, but it's true.

I didn't think about it until many years later. The baby born that night had become a man, and everybody had begun to talk about him. He had become a famous teacher and miracle worker. Joshua, Joshua, Joshua. That was all you heard.

"His voice is greater than that of Moses," said some.

"His touch is like the touch of God," said others.

"Surely he is the Messiah," many said.

"God has finally answered our prayers."

I wondered when I heard these things if it wasn't he, if the man they were talking about wasn't really the baby I had seen when I was a young man. He had the same name at least. Joshua. But Joshua, as you know, is a very common name. Oh, I was prosperous and powerful by this time—by some standards, at least—and I didn't have much time to think about it.

Sometimes at night, when I strolled on the porch of my great house, smelling the orange groves below, I pondered it. When I did, I went to bed with a strange stirring in my heart and dreamed beautiful dreams.

Then one day I was standing with some friends putting together a business deal when a buzz went through the market place. He was coming. Joshua of Nazareth was approaching Jericho, and throngs of people had already gone out to meet him.

I was electrified! Here. He was coming here! I had to see him. I had to be certain, if I possibly could. But how? The crowds were already gathering, and I was not a tall man. How could I possibly see him? The shouts heralding his approach drew near. I had an idea. On the other side of the marketplace, very near the gate of the city through which the highway comes, stands a gnarled old tree. It's still there today. I had sometimes sat beneath it to play dominoes with some of my friends. I knew it had a low fork in it, and that I could easily climb up into it, as I had often seen children do. My heart pounding with excitement, I raced to the tree and quickly climbed it.

It was just in time, for the shouts were drawing very near to the city wall. It was the most noise I had heard from a crowd since Caesar's proconsul had visited us several years before. I couldn't believe it. There I was, the chief tax collector of the entire region, a very important figure, perched in a tree, watching for the approach of the man whose name was on everybody's lips!

Suddenly, the crowd was spilling through the gate and along the street. I had been right to climb the tree. I would never have seen anything from below. Just then Joshua was passing beneath me, only a few feet from where I was sitting. And he stopped! Just like that, right in the midst of that great, flowing river of a crowd, he simply stopped. Everything around him came to a halt. He looked up into the tree and right into my eyes. I didn't have to be told. They were the very eyes into which I had gazed so long ago, in that corner of the shed where I saw the strange light and heard the heavenly music.

"Zacchaeus!" he was saying.

I almost didn't hear him, I was so caught up in the mystery of my own thoughts.

"Zacchaeus!"

Did he recognize me, after all those years? Had his eyes memorized my face that night? Had his little mind somehow recorded my name? How would he know me now, for I was two or three stones heavier and much older. And I had this beard, which I didn't have before.

"Zacchaeus," he said, "Come down! I want to have dinner with you! Let's go to your house!"

My house?! This enormously famous public figure—the Messiah—for I was sure of it, had been sure, I realized, ever since I'd heard of the man called Joshua. It had to be! He was God's chosen. And he was choosing me! He wanted to go home with me! After all those years, all that time.

Well, you know the rest. It turned my life around. We talked about everything, especially that night when he was born. Mary and Joseph had apparently told him everything about it—especially how I had gotten them a place to stay and had taken them something to eat. He thanked me for it. Imagine! The Savior of the world thanking me for what I had done.

I remembered that cask of gold the Eastern princes had brought. That night, in my home, I brought in an even larger cask and laid it at his feet.

"Behold, Lord," I said, "here is half of all I possess. It's yours—for the poor. If I have been unfair to anyone in all my years as a tax collector, I'm going to make it right, even if I have to repay each person I've wronged four times what I overcharged."

(Chuckling softly) I guess I still live that way. It's wonderful, you know. He taught me how, the way he gave himself to everybody. Life is so much richer this way. And on his birthday—oh yes, I still remember it;

I never could forget that—on his birthday I make it a special point to give away a lot of presents. It's my way of recalling—and of paying homage. It's the least I can do for a Child—and a Man—who has given so much for all of us.

Oh, please excuse me again. This old couple lost their son a few months ago, and things are hard for them right now. Maybe I can make things a little easier for them. You understand, I'm sure. . .